When Goodbye
is For Ever

So when you have to say goodbye
for ever to someone you love,
that is the saddest goodbye of all.

Some goodbyes that are for ever may be sad.

They can make you feel lost and lonely.

You may want to cry.

You may want someone to hug you and to comfort you until the pain and sadness go away.

Some goodbyes are for ever.

These goodbyes may be happy.

For in every ending there is also
a beginning, and some goodbyes
feel like happy new beginnings
and bright days.

Sometimes you don't.

There are longer goodbyes.
Sometimes you know how long
they will last.

From the time you were small,
you have learned to say goodbye.

These are little goodbyes
for a short time out of sight.

When Goodbye is For Ever

Lois Rock

Illustrated by Sheila Moxley

LION
Children's Books

Published by
Lion Publishing plc
Mayfield House, 256 Banbury Road,
Oxford OX2 7DH, England
www.lion-publishing.co.uk
ISBN 0 7459 4879 0

First edition 2004
1 3 5 7 9 10 8 6 4 2 0

A catalogue record for this book is available
from the British Library

Typeset in Revival565 BT
Printed and bound in Singapore

_____

_____

_____

But people do die.

Just as the flowers die,
just as the leaves die,
just as little creatures die.

In the end, everyone must die.

Sometimes, death comes
unexpectedly, like a frost
that kills the spring flowers.

It seems so unkind, so unfair.

Sometimes, death is expected,
just as winter follows autumn.

When someone you love has died, you may feel sadder and lonelier than ever before.

It may seem that you will cry for ever.

It may seem that the pain and sadness will never go away.

It may seem that no one can love you enough to help you.

Time will pass.

Into the empty space of goodbye will come the memories of happy times.

Just as morning follows night and spring follows winter, there will be new beginnings: new people to meet, new things to do.

The loved one who has died has
passed on to a new beginning.
They have gone to a new place that
is beyond what we can see, beyond
what we can fully understand.

That place we call heaven,
where God makes all things new;
where those we love are safe
in the love of God, as we are
safe in the love of God.

They will only be a little time
out of sight, for God's love will
gather us together for all eternity.

More books for young children from Lion Children's Books

The Goodbye Boat   *Mary Joslin and Claire St Louis Little*

Pip and the Edge of Heaven   *Elizabeth Liddle and Lara Jones*

The Shore Beyond   *Mary Joslin and Alison Jay*